MESSI, NEYMAR & SUÁREZ

THE BARCELONA TRIO

Abbeville Press Publishers

New York · London

A portion of this book's proceeds are donated to the **Hugo Bustamante AYSO Playership Fund**, a national scholarship program to help ensure that no child misses the chance to play AYSO Soccer. Donations to the fund cover the cost of registration and a uniform for a child in need.

Text by Illugi Jökulsson
Design and layout: Árni Torfason

For the English-language edition
Editor: Nicole Lanctot
Production manager: Louise Kurtz
Copy editor: Amy K. Hughes

PHOTOGRAPHY CREDITS

Getty Images: p. 2 (Alex Caparros), 6 (David Ramos), 11 (Central Press), 15 (Bagu Blanco), 17 (Jasper Juinen), 18 (Bryn Lennon), 19 (VI Images), 19 (Clive Brunskill), 20 (Jamie McDonald), 21 (Matthias Hangst), 21 (Clive Rose), 22 (Shaun Botterill), 22 (Jasper Juinen), 23 (Jasper Juinen), 24 (Gonzalo Arroyo Moreno), 27 (Lintao Zhang), 28 (Mike Hewitt), 29 (Lintao Zhang), 31 (Matthias Hangst), 36 (Gonzalo Arroyo Moreno), 39 (Shaun Botterill), 40 (David Ramos), 43 (David Ramos), 45 (Matthias Hangst), 48 (Robert Marquardt), 48 (David Ramos), 49 (Alex Livesey), 55 (Juan Mabromata/Afp), 56 (David Ramos), 57 (Denis Doyle), 58 (Denis Doyle), 59 (Denis Doyle), 61 (Denis Doyle), 61 (Harry Engels), 62 (Alex Caparros).

Shutterstock: p. 8 (Tupungato), 8 (kastianz), 9 (Eduardo Rivero), 10–11 (urbanbuzz), 25 (Natursports), 32 (Christian Bertrand), 33 (Andrew Barker), 35 (Natursports), 49 (Jefferson Bernardes), 50 (Maxisport), 50 (Natursports), 51 (mooinblack), 51 (mooinblack), 51 (Maxisport), 51 (Maxisport), 52 (Maxisport), 52 (Maxisport), 52 (Maxisport), 52 (Natursports), 53 (mooinblack), 53 (Maxisport), 53 (mooinblack), 53 (Celso Pupo), 53 (Maxisport), 60 (mooinblack), 60 (Natursports), 60 (almonfoto), 61 (mooinblack).

Wikimedia Commons: p. 7 ("CC No 01 Three Musketeers" by Chordboard)

Photographer unknown: p. 12, 17

First published in the United States of America in 2016 by Abbeville Press, 116 West 23rd Street, New York, NY 10011

First published in Iceland in 2015 by Sögur útgáfa, Fákafen 9, 108 Reykjavík, Iceland

First edition
10 9 8 7 6 5 4 3 2 1

ISBN 978-0-7892-1284-9

Library of Congress Cataloguing-in-Publication Data available upon request.

For bulk and premium sales and for text adoption procedures, write to Customer Service Manager, Abbeville Press, 116 West 23rd Street, New York, NY 10011, or call 1-800-ARTBOOK.

Visit Abbeville Press online at www.abbeville.com.

CONTENTS

When the Uruguayan striker Luis Suárez joined Futbol Club Barcelona in the summer of 2014, it was clear that history was in the making. The magnificently skillful Suárez was to be the third member of a spectacular forward line, joining the Argentinean great Lionel Messi and the precocious Brazilian supertalent Neymar.

The move turned out to be historic indeed. The three superstars, often referred to by their initials as "MSN," scored a whopping 122 goals combined during the 2014–2015 season. They dovetailed perfectly and were the driving force behind Barcelona's triple win of the La Liga, Copa del Rey, and Champions League titles. And these Three Musketeers would soon show that this was just the beginning!

THE THREE MUSKETEERS
122 GOALS

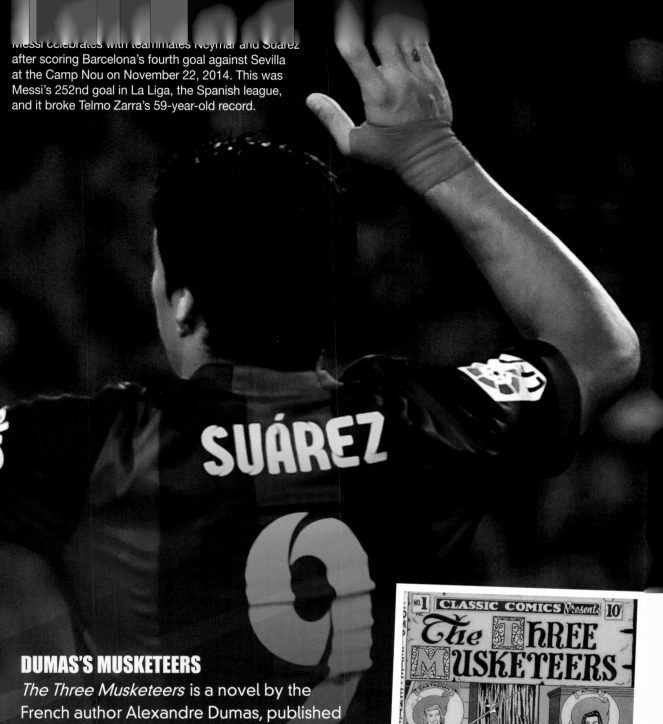

Messi celebrates with teammates Neymar and Suárez after scoring Barcelona's fourth goal against Sevilla at the Camp Nou on November 22, 2014. This was Messi's 252nd goal in La Liga, the Spanish league, and it broke Telmo Zarra's 59-year-old record.

DUMAS'S MUSKETEERS

The Three Musketeers is a novel by the French author Alexandre Dumas, published in 1844, about the adventures of three swashbucklers during the 1600s in France. The Musketeers, named Athos, Porthos, and Aramis, are adept at using sword and pistols. But above all, they are merry, noble, and true to one another—not to mention inventive and full of surprises. Just like Messi, Suárez,

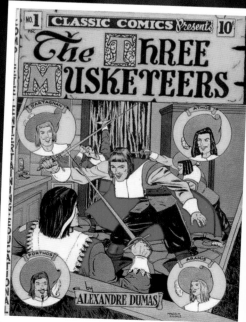

SOUTH AMERICA

VENEZUELA
GUYANA
SURI-
FRENCH GUIANA
COLOMBIA

ECUADOR

AMAZON
Manaus

PERU

BRAZIL

ANDES MOUNTAINS

BOLIVIA

Brasília
Belo Horizonte

PARAGUAY

Rio de Janeiro
São Paolo
Curitiba

CHILE

Porto Alegre

SOUTH ATLANTIC OCEAN

ARGENTINA

URUGUAY

Buenos Aires
Montevideo

A jungle in the Serra dos Orgãos National Park, near Rio de Janeiro, Brazil.

A beautiful beach in Colonia del Sacramento, Uruguay.

URUGUAY is almost a microstate compared to its giant neighbors. Yet it is 68,000 square miles in area, slightly larger than Florida. With only 3.3 million inhabitants, Uruguay is by far the least populous nation ever to win the World Cup. The country boasts an astonishingly good record at international soccer, winning the World Cup twice and making it to the semifinals three times, most recently in 2010. Uruguay has also won the Copa América 15 times, more than any other team. It is also the smallest country (by population) to have taken home Olympic gold in any team sport—which it has done twice in men's soccer!

"Uruguay" means "bird river."

BRAZIL is the fifth largest country in the world. At nearly 3.3 million square miles, it is almost as big as the contiguous United States. Much of the world's largest expanse of rain forest, traversed by the mighty Amazon River, is found inside the country's borders. Sadly, the Amazon rain forest has deteriorated in recent years.

Brazil is sixth in the world when it comes to population, with nearly 204 million people. Brazilians are famous for their style of play, known as samba soccer, with its emphasis on beautiful interplay and graceful movements in attack. However, the Brazilian national team is also expected to win every competition it takes part in, and samba soccer has declined as an ever-increasing emphasis on results has won out over grace and harmony.

"Brazil" means "redwood tree."

ARGENTINA is a huge country, even if it covers less than half the area of Brazil. It covers over 1 million square miles—almost the combined area of Alaska, Texas, and California—and is home to 43 million people. Argentina's geography is very diverse, ranging from jungles in the north to the vast plains called Las Pampas to the frosty Tierra del Fuego region in the extreme south.

Argentineans play soccer with great passion and fighting spirit. They often do not care about the means to victory, yet still believe the Argentinean soccer style to be the most beautiful and artistic.

"Argentina" means "silver country."

Sandstone, eroded into strange formations by the wind, cover the Pampas in Ischigualasto, Argentina. The area is a UNESCO World Heritage Site.

WORLD CUP CHAMPIONSHIPS

None of our Three Musketeers has yet won the World Cup, but the teams from their home countries have won it a combined nine times.

1930 URUGUAY
1934 Italy
1938 Italy
1950 URUGUAY
1954 West Germany
1958 BRAZIL
1962 BRAZIL
1966 England
1970 BRAZIL
1974 West Germany
1978 ARGENTINA
1982 Italy
1986 ARGENTINA
1990 West Germany
1994 BRAZIL
1998 France
2002 BRAZIL
2006 Italy
2010 Spain
2014 Germany

World Cup in Uruguay, 1930
URUGUAY

The first world tournament was held in Uruguay, and the hosts beat Argentina 4–2 in an eventful final match. Pedro Cea (1900–1970) turned the tide in the final match when he scored in the 57th minute to tie the score at 2–2. He was the leading scorer for Uruguay, with five goals.

World Cup in Brazil, 1950
URUGUAY

The Brazilians had been certain that with their overwhelming attacking force they would win their first World Cup victory, but the Uruguayans pulled off a surprise win, 2–1. During the legendary final match, Uruguay captain Obdulio Varela (1917–1996) encouraged his men in the face of 200,000 Brazilians cheering on the home team in Maracanã Stadium.

World Cup in Sweden, 1958
BRAZIL

The Brazilians finally claimed World Cup gold, with a resounding 5–2 victory over Sweden in the final in 1958. Pelé (b. 1940) was 17 years old and totally unknown outside Brazil when he became the sensation of the Swedish World Cup. He scored two goals in the final match.

World Cup in Chile, 1962
BRAZIL

The Brazilians defended their title rather easily, with a 3–1 victory over Czechoslovakia in the final. Garrincha (1933–1983) was Brazilian samba soccer incarnate, an outrageously talented attacking player. With Pelé out because of injury, Garrincha ably filled the void.

Best player: Garrincha, in Brazil.

World Cup in Mexico, 1970
BRAZIL

In one of the most exciting World Cups in history, Brazil brought home its third gold, with a magnificent 4–1 final victory over Italy. Pelé was foremost among equals in a fantastic Brazilian team and ensured his place among the all-time greats.

World Cup in Argentina, 1978
ARGENTINA

On their home turf, the aggressive and opportunistic Argentineans defeated a skillful Netherlands team 3–1, after extra time. Argentina's Mario Kempes (b. 1954) was the tournament's leading scorer and made two goals in the final.

World Cup in Mexico, 1986
ARGENTINA

The memorable competition of 1986 ended with Argentina beating West Germany 3–2 in a thrilling game. Diego Maradona (b. 1960) brilliantly led the Argentineans— and did not hesitate to score with his hand when the opportunity arose!

World Cup in United States, 1994
BRAZIL

After the great teams of 1982 and 1986 underperformed at the World Cup, the Brazilians were growing tired of waiting for their fourth gold. The class of 1994 may not have been as scintillating to watch, but it got the job done, beating Italy on penalties in the final. Romário (b. 1966), a flamboyant attacker, scored five goals for Brazil.

World Cup in Japan/South Korea, 2002
BRAZIL

In the first World Cup of the 21st century, Brazilian attacking geniuses Ronaldo, Ronaldinho, and Rivaldo were unleashed to beat Germany 2–0 in the final. Ronaldo (b. 1976) was the tournament's top scorer, with eight goals, and scored both of the goals in the final match.

Leo
THE GENIUS

Lionel Messi joined Barcelona's famous youth academy at age 13 and is its greatest achievement.

On June 24, 1987, one year (almost to the day) after Argentina won the World Cup in Mexico, with the fantastic Maradona leading the way, a boy was born in the Argentinean city of Rosario. This youngster was destined to become Maradona's successor as one of the greatest players in the history of soccer. He may yet deliver Argentina its third World Cup victory. His parents, Jorge Messi and Celia Cuccittini, named him Lionel Andrés.

Rosario is an old city with about 1.2 million inhabitants. Lionel's father worked in a steel factory, while his mother did cleaning work. Little Lionel, known as Leo, was their third son, and a daughter was to arrive later. The family did not have much money to spare but enough to lead a decent life. Leo's father and older brothers were soccer enthusiasts, like most Argentineans, but as a toddler Leo did not seem interested in the sport. But at the age of four, he joined his father and brothers as they were playing outside the family home. They were shocked when he displayed amazing skills, although he had never touched a soccer ball before.

Not long afterward, Leo's grandmother brought the little boy to his brothers' soccer practice. She often babysat the children, and Leo was very fond of her. For fun, Leo was offered a chance to join in the game, playing on the wing so he could be taken off the field if the older boys intimidated him. But the little boy amazed everyone by repeatedly dribbling the ball through the big boys, while his grandmother and the coach stood gaping at the sight.

In the next few years, it became increasingly obvious that Leo Messi had extraordinary talent. He was quiet and did not seem very passionate, but when the ball was at his feet he became unstoppable. However, Leo remained very small, and soon it was apparent that his failure to grow was from a hormone deficiency. It was predicted that without regular hormone injections, he might reach a height of only four feet eight inches—which would prevent him from maximizing his potential as a soccer player. But the injections were far too expensive for the Messi family to afford.

Rosario's leading soccer club, Newell's Old Boys, took Leo under its wing and paid for his injections for a while, until an economic collapse in Argentina led the club to withdraw its support. Talent scouts who had seen Leo play put his father, Jorge, into contact with sports agents in Barcelona in the Spanish province of Catalonia. At the age of 13, Leo and his father went to Barcelona, where the manager Carles Rexach decided after only minutes of watching him play to sign the boy. A contract, however, was not drawn up until Messi's agents warned Rexach that his club's archrival, Real Madrid, was preparing to sign the young Argentinean. Rexach wasted no more time, writing a contract on a paper napkin and signing it. Leo Messi had become a Barcelona player!

BARCELONA
"MORE THAN A CLUB"

Futbol Club Barcelona was founded in 1899 by a Swiss businessman, Joan Gamper, who had settled in the city. The club was soon among the best in Spain, and won the championship in the first season of La Liga, the country's top division, in 1929. The club became known for great passion and for emphasizing style of play rather than results only. FC Barcelona is also a symbol of the strength of Catalonia, whose people crave autonomy, and in some cases even independence from Spain. Regional pride has led to the saying that Barça is *més que un club*—"more than a [soccer] club."

Although many of the greatest players in the world have played for Barcelona over the years, for a long time the club was eclipsed by the trophy haul of Real Madrid. But this started to change around 1990. The Dutch star Johan Cruyff had played for Barcelona in his prime and was now the team's head coach. He assembled the so-called Dream Team, which began to gather awards at a furious pace. Since 1991, Barça has won far more championship trophies than its chief rival, Real.

Cruyff played a part in Barcelona's emphasis on youth development at La Masia, the facility where the club's up-and-coming prospects are headquartered. At La Masia, young soccer players learn "tiki-taka," the great style of play that has been a hallmark of FC Barcelona and is based chiefly on interplay and short passes. The embodiment of this fantastic institution is the boy from Rosario, Leo Messi.

Messi leaves two Getafe players in his wake on April 18, 2007, at the Camp Nou. He had not yet turned 20. All in all, he shook off five defenders before he scored.

A GLITTERING START FOR MESSI

On October 16, 2004, 17-year-old Leo Messi played his first game for Barcelona in La Liga against neighboring team Espanyol. On May 1, 2005, he scored his first league goal, against Albacete. Barça manager Frank Rijkaard trusted his young player, who would play an ever-larger part in the coming years. Word began to spread about the Barcelona prodigy, and on April 18, 2007, Messi became world famous when he scored a stunning goal (his second) against Getafe in the Spanish competition Copa del Rey. He started his run from the middle of the field, surged past five rushing defenders, dodged the goalkeeper, and rounded off the play with a firm goal. It happened to be almost an exact copy of Diego Maradona's legendary "Goal of the Century" against England in the 1986 World Cup. It was clear that Messi was his countryman's worthy successor!

When Pep Guardiola became the Barça head coach in 2008, Messi and Barcelona began their run of success in earnest. The following year Messi was chosen Europe's best player, claiming the Ballon d'Or, or Golden Ball, for the first time—but not the last!

Luis
THE STREET URCHIN

Two hundred miles away from Rosario, where Leo Messi grew up, lies the Uruguayan city of Salto. With a population of 100,000 people, the city has a quiet reputation. Half a year before Messi was born in Rosario, the fourth of seven sons was born to the Suárez family in Salto. He was named Luis.

Luis's parents were not people of great means; his father was a doorman and his mother was a homemaker. When Luis was seven years old, the family moved to the capital city of Montevideo, which has 1.3 million people and a more colorful street life.

Luis had already caused a stir with his soccer talent in Salto. At the age of four, he was said to run faster with a ball than without it. In Montevideo, he started playing in the streets with other boys. These matches were not for the faint of heart— the young soccer enthusiasts did not always hold the rules in high regard! Luis soon developed an appetite for goals and learned to fight hard to achieve them.

When he was not yet 10 years old, Luis started training at a small club called Urreta. He was on the substitutes' bench in his first game against a strong team in his age group. His side was losing when Luis was called to the pitch. He quickly scored three goals, and Urreta won the game. A scout from the youth division of Nacional, a major club in Montevideo, soon spotted the young player. "He had incredible ability for someone of that age," the scout remembers. "You could always tell he was going to be a great player."

Suárez soon started playing for the Nacional youth team, but his early years there were turbulent. His parents had gotten divorced, and his mother was having a hard time taking care of seven children. On one occasion Suárez was not able to take his place on a youth team because he could not afford proper soccer shoes. He had a fiery temper and was often shown a yellow penalty card or even a red. For a while he quit soccer, but Nacional's trainers persuaded him to rejoin. They were confident that if Suárez could learn to control his temper, he would become an outstanding player.

Suárez soon decided to commit fully to harnessing his talent. At the age of 18,

Messi celebrates with teammates Neymar and Suárez after scoring Barcelona's fourth goal against Sevilla at the Camp Nou on November 22, 2014. This was Messi's 252nd goal in La Liga, the Spanish league, and it broke Telmo Zarra's 59-year-old record.

DUMAS'S MUSKETEERS

The Three Musketeers is a novel by the French author Alexandre Dumas, published in 1844, about the adventures of three swashbucklers during the 1600s in France. The Musketeers, named Athos, Porthos, and Aramis, are adept at using sword and pistols. But above all, they are merry, noble, and true to one another—not to mention inventive and full of surprises. Just like Messi, Suárez,

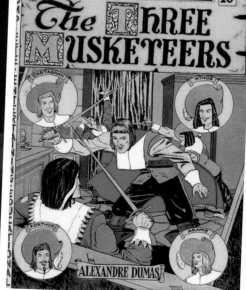

SOUTH AMERICA

VENEZUELA
GUYANA
SURI-
FRENCH GUIANA
COLOMBIA
ECUADOR
AMAZON
Manaus
PERU
BRAZIL
BOLIVIA
Brasília
Belo Horizonte
PARAGUAY
Rio de Janeiro
São Paolo
CHILE
Curitiba
ANDES MOUNTAINS
Porto Alegre
SOUTH ATLANTIC OCEAN
ARGENTINA
URUGUAY
Buenos Aires
Montevideo

A jungle in the Serra dos Orgãos National Park, near Rio de Janeiro, Brazil.

A beautiful beach in Colonia del Sacramento, Uruguay.

URUGUAY is almost a microstate compared to its giant neighbors. Yet it is 68,000 square miles in area, slightly larger than Florida. With only 3.3 million inhabitants, Uruguay is by far the least populous nation ever to win the World Cup. The country boasts an astonishingly good record at international soccer, winning the World Cup twice and making it to the semifinals three times, most recently in 2010. Uruguay has also won the Copa América 15 times, more than any other team. It is also the smallest country (by population) to have taken home Olympic gold in any team sport—which it has done twice in men's soccer!

"Uruguay" means "bird river."

BRAZIL is the fifth largest country in the world. At nearly 3.3 million square miles, it is almost as big as the contiguous United States. Much of the world's largest expanse of rain forest, traversed by the mighty Amazon River, is found inside the country's borders. Sadly, the Amazon rain forest has deteriorated in recent years.

Brazil is sixth in the world when it comes to population, with nearly 204 million people. Brazilians are famous for their style of play, known as samba soccer, with its emphasis on beautiful interplay and graceful movements in attack. However, the Brazilian national team is also expected to win every competition it takes part in, and samba soccer has declined as an ever-increasing emphasis on results has won out over grace and harmony.

"Brazil" means "redwood tree."

ARGENTINA is a huge country, even if it covers less than half the area of Brazil. It covers over 1 million square miles—almost the combined area of Alaska, Texas, and California—and is home to 43 million people. Argentina's geography is very diverse, ranging from jungles in the north to the vast plains called Las Pampas to the frosty Tierra del Fuego region in the extreme south.

Argentineans play soccer with great passion and fighting spirit. They often do not care about the means to victory, yet still believe the Argentinean soccer style to be the most beautiful and artistic.

"Argentina" means "silver country."

Sandstone, eroded into strange formations by the wind, cover the Pampas in Ischigualasto, Argentina. The area is a UNESCO World Heritage Site.

WORLD CUP CHAMPIONSHIPS

None of our Three Musketeers has yet won the World Cup, but the teams from their home countries have won it a combined nine times.

1930 URUGUAY
1934 Italy
1938 Italy
1950 URUGUAY
1954 West Germany
1958 BRAZIL
1962 BRAZIL
1966 England
1970 BRAZIL
1974 West Germany
1978 ARGENTINA
1982 Italy
1986 ARGENTINA
1990 West Germany
1994 BRAZIL
1998 France
2002 BRAZIL
2006 Italy
2010 Spain
2014 Germany

World Cup in Uruguay, 1930
URUGUAY

The first world tournament was held in Uruguay, and the hosts beat Argentina 4–2 in an eventful final match. Pedro Cea (1900–1970) turned the tide in the final match when he scored in the 57th minute to tie the score at 2–2. He was the leading scorer for Uruguay, with five goals.

World Cup in Brazil, 1950
URUGUAY

The Brazilians had been certain that with their overwhelming attacking force they would win their first World Cup victory, but the Uruguayans pulled off a surprise win, 2–1. During the legendary final match, Uruguay captain Obdulio Varela (1917–1996) encouraged his men in the face of 200,000 Brazilians cheering on the home team in Maracanã Stadium.

World Cup in Sweden, 1958
BRAZIL

The Brazilians finally claimed World Cup gold, with a resounding 5–2 victory over Sweden in the final in 1958. Pelé (b. 1940) was 17 years old and totally unknown outside Brazil when he became the sensation of the Swedish World Cup. He scored two goals in the final match.

World Cup in Chile, 1962
BRAZIL

The Brazilians defended their title rather easily, with a 3–1 victory over Czechoslovakia in the final. Garrincha (1933–1983) was Brazilian samba soccer incarnate, an outrageously talented attacking player. With Pelé out because of injury, Garrincha ably filled the void.

Best player: Garrincha, in Brazil.

World Cup in Mexico, 1970
BRAZIL

In one of the most exciting World Cups in history, Brazil brought home its third gold, with a magnificent 4–1 final victory over Italy. Pelé was foremost among equals in a fantastic Brazilian team and ensured his place among the all-time greats.

World Cup in Argentina, 1978
ARGENTINA

On their home turf, the aggressive and opportunistic Argentineans defeated a skillful Netherlands team 3–1, after extra time. Argentina's Mario Kempes (b. 1954) was the tournament's leading scorer and made two goals in the final.

World Cup in Mexico, 1986
ARGENTINA

The memorable competition of 1986 ended with Argentina beating West Germany 3–2 in a thrilling game. Diego Maradona (b. 1960) brilliantly led the Argentineans— and did not hesitate to score with his hand when the opportunity arose!

World Cup in United States, 1994
BRAZIL

After the great teams of 1982 and 1986 underperformed at the World Cup, the Brazilians were growing tired of waiting for their fourth gold. The class of 1994 may not have been as scintillating to watch, but it got the job done, beating Italy on penalties in the final. Romário (b. 1966), a flamboyant attacker, scored five goals for Brazil.

World Cup in Japan/South Korea, 2002
BRAZIL

In the first World Cup of the 21st century, Brazilian attacking geniuses Ronaldo, Ronaldinho, and Rivaldo were unleashed to beat Germany 2–0 in the final. Ronaldo (b. 1976) was the tournament's top scorer, with eight goals, and scored both of the goals in the final match.

Leo
THE GENIUS

Lionel Messi joined Barcelona's famous youth academy at age 13 and is its greatest achievement.

On June 24, 1987, one year (almost to the day) after Argentina won the World Cup in Mexico, with the fantastic Maradona leading the way, a boy was born in the Argentinean city of Rosario. This youngster was destined to become Maradona's successor as one of the greatest players in the history of soccer. He may yet deliver Argentina its third World Cup victory. His parents, Jorge Messi and Celia Cuccittini, named him Lionel Andrés.

Rosario is an old city with about 1.2 million inhabitants. Lionel's father worked in a steel factory, while his mother did cleaning work. Little Lionel, known as Leo, was their third son, and a daughter was to arrive later. The family did not have much money to spare but enough to lead a decent life. Leo's father and older brothers were soccer enthusiasts, like most Argentineans, but as a toddler Leo did not seem interested in the sport. But at the age of four, he joined his father and brothers as they were playing outside the family home. They were shocked when he displayed amazing skills, although he had never touched a soccer ball before.

Not long afterward, Leo's grandmother brought the little boy to his brothers' soccer practice. She often babysat the children, and Leo was very fond of her. For fun, Leo was offered a chance to join in the game, playing on the wing so he could be taken off the field if the older boys intimidated him. But the little boy amazed everyone by repeatedly dribbling the ball through the big boys, while his grandmother and the coach stood gaping at the sight.

In the next few years, it became increasingly obvious that Leo Messi had extraordinary talent. He was quiet and did not seem very passionate, but when the ball was at his feet he became unstoppable. However, Leo remained very small, and soon it was apparent that his failure to grow was from a hormone deficiency. It was predicted that without regular hormone injections, he might reach a height of only four feet eight inches— which would prevent him from maximizing

his potential as a soccer player. But the injections were far too expensive for the Messi family to afford.

Rosario's leading soccer club, Newell's Old Boys, took Leo under its wing and paid for his injections for a while, until an economic collapse in Argentina led the club to withdraw its support. Talent scouts who had seen Leo play put his father, Jorge, into contact with sports agents in Barcelona in the Spanish province of Catalonia. At the age of 13, Leo and his father went to Barcelona, where the manager Carles Rexach decided after only minutes of watching him play to sign the boy. A contract, however, was not drawn up until Messi's agents warned Rexach that his club's archrival, Real Madrid, was preparing to sign the young Argentinean. Rexach wasted no more time, writing a contract on a paper napkin and signing it. Leo Messi had become a Barcelona player!

BARCELONA
"MORE THAN A CLUB"

Futbol Club Barcelona was founded in 1899 by a Swiss businessman, Joan Gamper, who had settled in the city. The club was soon among the best in Spain, and won the championship in the first season of La Liga, the country's top division, in 1929. The club became known for great passion and for emphasizing style of play rather than results only. FC Barcelona is also a symbol of the strength of Catalonia, whose people crave autonomy, and in some cases even independence from Spain. Regional pride has led to the saying that Barça is *més que un club*—"more than a [soccer] club."

Although many of the greatest players in the world have played for Barcelona over the years, for a long time the club was eclipsed by the trophy haul of Real Madrid. But this started to change around 1990. The Dutch star Johan Cruyff had played for Barcelona in his prime and was now the team's head coach. He assembled the so-called Dream Team, which began to gather awards at a furious pace. Since 1991, Barça has won far more championship trophies than its chief rival, Real.

Cruyff played a part in Barcelona's emphasis on youth development at La Masia, the facility where the club's up-and-coming prospects are headquartered. At La Masia, young soccer players learn "tiki-taka," the great style of play that has been a hallmark of FC Barcelona and is based chiefly on interplay and short passes. The embodiment of this fantastic institution is the boy from Rosario, Leo Messi.

Messi leaves two Getafe players in his wake on April 18, 2007, at the Camp Nou. He had not yet turned 20. All in all, he shook off five defenders before he scored.

A fountain in Salto's main square.

Suárez at a young age.

he played his first game for Nacional in Uruguay's top division. In June 2006, the team won the national championship. Suárez scored two goals in two final matches against opponents Rocha.

Scouts from the Dutch club Groningen showed up at one of Nacional's games to track another player they were interested in signing. But the 19-year-old Suárez caught their eye, and it took only one game for them to make him an offer. Groningen swiftly secured a contract with the goal-getter from Salto. Although Groningen was not a huge club, Suárez was anxious to get to Europe. Not only would it be easier for him to attract the attention of the major clubs, but he would also be closer to the girl he was in love with! (See page 49.)

On August 5, 2010, daughter Delfina was born to Sofia and Luis Suárez. Three years later, on September 26, 2013, her brother, Benjamin, arrived.

SUÁREZ
THE NETHERLANDS AND LIVERPOOL

In the summer of 2006, Luis Suárez arrived in the Netherlands after signing with Groningen, a middle-of-the-pack team in Eredivisie, the country's top division. The 19-year-old didn't make a big splash at first. He had problems adjusting and controlling his temper, but before long the goals started flowing. The high-ranking club Ajax Amsterdam signed him in the summer of 2007, and with Ajax, Suárez began to flourish. He improved steadily, proving to be a combative goal machine, and in the 2009–2010 season scored 35 goals in 33 Eredivisie league games. The fiery Uruguayan was clearly on his way to becoming one of the elite strikers of the game. The biggest European clubs started paying attention—but Suárez was problematic. He constantly received penalty cards and even suspensions. In November 2010, he bit an opponent for the first time.

Liverpool, the flailing giant of the English Premier League, sorely needed a goal scorer to get back among the top teams. In January 2011, Suárez showed

spectacular history of music and soccer. Suárez played for Liverpool for three and a half seasons. During this time he became world famous—for a string of controversies as much as his peerless performances on the field. Some claimed that Suárez was simply uncontrollable and would always be a problem. Liverpool, however, supported him through good times and bad. Suárez, his supporters insisted, was a perfect gentleman off the playing field; in due time they believed he was bound to gain control of his aggression on the field.

Suárez and his Groningen teammates celebrate a goal against the Dutch team Vitesse Arnhem on October 1, 2006.

CONTROVERSIAL INCIDENTS

Controversy surrounded Suárez while he played for Ajax in 2010.

JULY 2, 2010:

Suárez had been playing impeccably for Uruguay at the World Cup in South Africa. In the quarterfinal against Ghana, the score was tied at 1–1 in extra time, when Suárez deliberately blocked a shot with his hands, preventing Ghana from scoring a decisive goal. The Ghanaians failed to score from the resulting penalty kick, and Uruguay went on to win on penalties. An unapologetic Suárez declared, "I made the best save of the tournament."

NOVEMBER 20, 2010:

Playing for Ajax, Suárez bites the Dutch midfielder Otman Bakkal of PSV Eindhoven. Suárez is suspended for seven games. While he is suspended, he joins Liverpool at the beginning of the 2011.

OCTOBER 15, 2011:

Playing for Liverpool, Suárez is accused of racially abusing Patrice Evra of Manchester United by repeatedly calling him "negro" as they tussled in Manchester's penalty area. Suárez tried to downplay the incident by claiming that in Uruguay the word is not used in a pejorative sense and that his grandfather was black. Nevertheless, Suárez is fined and banned for eight games.

FEBRUARY 11, 2012:

Suárez refuses to shake Patrice Evra's hand before the first Liverpool–Manchester game since the racial abuse incident the previous fall. He later apologizes.

Suárez and Patrice Evra struggle for control of the ball, which led to racial abuse charges in the Liverpool vs. Manchester United game on October 15, 2011.

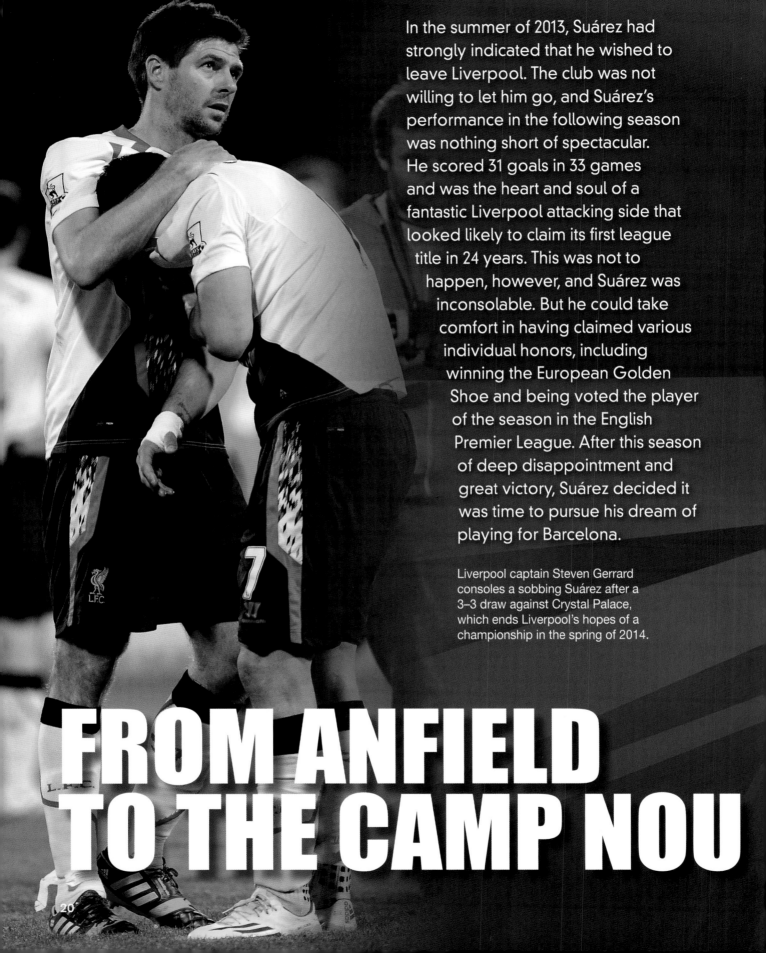

In the summer of 2013, Suárez had strongly indicated that he wished to leave Liverpool. The club was not willing to let him go, and Suárez's performance in the following season was nothing short of spectacular. He scored 31 goals in 33 games and was the heart and soul of a fantastic Liverpool attacking side that looked likely to claim its first league title in 24 years. This was not to happen, however, and Suárez was inconsolable. But he could take comfort in having claimed various individual honors, including winning the European Golden Shoe and being voted the player of the season in the English Premier League. After this season of deep disappointment and great victory, Suárez decided it was time to pursue his dream of playing for Barcelona.

Liverpool captain Steven Gerrard consoles a sobbing Suárez after a 3–3 draw against Crystal Palace, which ends Liverpool's hopes of a championship in the spring of 2014.

FROM ANFIELD TO THE CAMP NOU

MORE CONTROVERSIAL INCIDENTS

APRIL 21, 2013:

Playing for Liverpool against Chelsea, Suárez bites the Serbian defender Branislav Ivanović. The referee fails to notice the incident, but Suárez is subsequently banned for 10 games.

JUNE 24, 2014:

In the final game of the group stage of the World Cup in Brazil, Suárez bites the Italian defender Giorgio Chiellini. The referee misses the incident, and Uruguay eventually wins 1–0. After the game Suárez initially pleads innocent but eventually receives a nine-game international ban and a four-month ban from playing altogether.

Suárez checks whether a tooth has come loose after biting Giorgio Chiellini.

Branislav Ivanović and Suárez shake hands before Chelsea plays Liverpool.

LUIS SUÁREZ I

One of the Barcelona legends of earlier times was a Spanish player also named Luis Suárez. He played for the club from 1955 to 1961, and in 1960 he became the first Barcelona player to receive the Golden Ball. Suárez was a midfielder, renowned for his graceful and elegant play. This is the kind of soccer that Barça fans have always insisted upon!

THE GOLDEN BOY

While Luis Suárez gradually made his name—playing at Groningen and Ajax in the Netherlands and later Liverpool—Messi, it might be said, started at the top in Barcelona and has been there ever since! In his early days, brilliant players such as Xavi, Andrés Iniesta, Carles Puyol, Ronaldinho, and Samuel Eto'o were the mainstays of the team, but Messi soon grew in importance. He won the Golden Ball for the first time, for the 2008–2009 season, after scoring Barça's second goal in a 2–0 victory over Manchester United in the UEFA (Union of European Football Associations) Champions League final. Although Argentina's performance at the 2010 World Cup in South Africa was a disappointment, Messi kept scoring for his club at an astonishing rate—and racking up trophies for his ever-growing collection!

In the UEFA Champions League final of 2011, Messi again scored for Barça against Manchester United, bringing home a 3–1 victory. He won the Golden Ball four years in a row, which was a previously unheard of feat. Messi's performances in these years were out of this world!

Maradona consoles Messi after Argentina's devastating World Cup loss to Germany on July 3, 2010.

Xavi, Iniesta, and Messi celebrate after Iniesta scores for Barça.

Pep Guardiola was a tough and decisive midfielder in his prime year as a Barcelona player. After he became coach he elevated the tiki-taka style of play, with the support of players like Messi. Here Guardiola instructs Messi in a game against Real Madrid on December 13, 2008. Barça won 2–0.

Messi celebrates Barcelona's third goal against Real Madrid on March 23, 2014. Cristiano Ronaldo and Ángel Di María are not happy, while Neymar catches his breath after his teammate's feat.

THE GREAT RIVAL

Ever since Messi emerged as a football phenomenon, fans have debated his rivalry with Cristiano Ronaldo, the Portuguese star of Real Madrid. Both are outstanding players, but by most yardsticks Messi holds an edge in goal scoring and assists. He is also considered a more creative player than his main rival.

The two players have taken turns winning the Golden Ball award since 2008. Ronaldo won the award that year, but then Messi took possession, winning in 2009, 2010, 2011, and 2012. In 2013 and 2014, Messi seemed in a slump by his own incredible standards, and Ronaldo took home the award in both years. But Messi was certainly not finished, as he proved by securing the Ballon d'Or again after a spectacular performance in 2014–2015, the first season of the MSN trio at the Camp Nou.

Messi scores against Atlético Madrid on December 16, 2012.

MESSI'S WONDER YEAR

In Barcelona's 2011–2012 season, Messi was nearly unstoppable in front of any opponents' goal. He rarely played a game without scoring, ending the season with 73 goals in 60 games. And in the calendar year 2012, in 69 official games Messi scored 91 goals! Twelve of those goals came in international matches for Argentina, and 79 goals were for Barça.

Neymar
THE NEW PELÉ?

By 2010, Brazilian soccer fans were growing worried. Heroes of the national team such as Ronaldo and Ronaldinho were aging. For years the Brazilians had depended on an ever-productive supply line of new talent, but now the machine seemed to be failing. Brazilian soccer clubs developed an endless number of perfectly decent and powerful players, but bona fide geniuses were suddenly in short supply.

Just then, a young man stepped forward who seemed capable of fulfilling his countrymen's dreams.

Neymar da Silva Santos Jr. was born in a suburb of the vast metropolis of São Paulo on February 5, 1992. As it happens, he shares a birthday with soccer superstars Cristiano Ronaldo and Carlos Tevez. Neymar came from a family of modest means. His father had played soccer for lower-level clubs but had to retire early due to injuries and became a mechanic. Neymar's younger sister was born in 1996.

When Neymar Sr. noticed his son's considerable soccer talent, he encouraged the boy constantly. This was, however, hardly necessary, since the eager young player was, from the outset, determined to make it in the game. Neymar Jr. was blessed with speed, acceleration, and mesmerizing ball control.

In fact, it was an experienced scout

Scan and watch!

Neymar's first goal for Santos, March 16, 2009.

Neymar being interviewed at age 13.

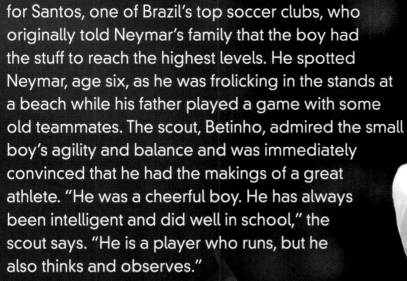

for Santos, one of Brazil's top soccer clubs, who originally told Neymar's family that the boy had the stuff to reach the highest levels. He spotted Neymar, age six, as he was frolicking in the stands at a beach while his father played a game with some old teammates. The scout, Betinho, admired the small boy's agility and balance and was immediately convinced that he had the makings of a great athlete. "He was a cheerful boy. He has always been intelligent and did well in school," the scout says. "He is a player who runs, but he also thinks and observes."

Neymar started training with a local team, but at the age of 11 he joined the Santos youth squad in São Paulo. When he was 14 he tried out for Real Madrid in Spain, impressing the coaches with his speed and skill. He was offered a youth contract, but Santos, not wanting to lose him, paid a large amount to keep him in São Paulo.

In March 2009, Neymar played his first professional-level game for Santos, and only a week later he scored his first goal, against Mogi Mirim. While running at speed he received the ball perfectly, slid through the defense, and scored. It was typical for Neymar: fast and precise! In the following year he made a name for himself, scoring 42 times in 60 games. The goals were often spectacular, but he also showed a great maturity and understanding of the game. Brazilians praised their luck and hoped that a worthy successor to Pelé had emerged!

Neymar playing for Santos in 2011.

Neymar
TO EUROPE

In the spring of 2010, when Neymar was still only 18 years old, the FIFA World Cup in South Africa was approaching. A campaign was underway to petition the Brazilian national team's head coach, Dunga, to pick the talented teenager for the roster. Dunga, however, decided Neymar was not ready, and the team went to the cup without him. Maybe things would have turned out differently for Brazil had Neymar played. The team struggled to score goals in a crucial match and was eliminated in the quarterfinal.

But Neymar had no problems scoring. He was instrumental in a great run of success for Santos from 2009 to 2012, when the team won the very tough São Paulo regional competition for three years running. Santos also won the Brazilian Cup with Neymar. In June 2011, Santos played two final matches against the Uruguayan club Peñarol in the Copa Libertadores, the South American equivalent of the UEFA Champions League. Neymar had been the main force in getting Santos to the finals, and he scored the first goal in his team's decisive 2–1 victory over Peñarol. Santos' last stop that year was the Club World Cup in Japan, where the team finished second.

Europe's biggest clubs had been eyeing the South American star throughout these years. Chelsea and Real Madrid had both declared their interest. But by the summer of 2013, it was clear that Neymar was headed for Barcelona.

Neymar in action during a league match on April 25, 2015, against Barcelona's local rivals Espanyol.

Neymar celebrates after Brazil beat Chile in the first knockout round of the 2014 World Cup.

Neymar has attracted attention not only for his soccer talent and his vivacious nature—his hairstyle has also brought him considerable attention, too. In his younger days, Neymar constantly changed his hairstyle, and became a fashion trendsetter. Young boys around the world would drop into their local barbershop with a recent picture of Neymar and request the same haircut.

2014 WORLD CUP

The first season Messi and Neymar played together at Barça did not entirely go as planned. They became good friends and struck up a fruitful partnership on the soccer field, but the team failed to win any trophies. Under coach Pep Guardiola, Barça won 14 trophies in four years, but when Pep left in 2012 and Gerardo Martino took over for 2013–2014, a slump set in. The club finished second in La Liga, lost the final of the Copa del Rey to Real Madrid, and was eliminated in the quarterfinal of the Champions League by Atlético Madrid. Messi kept scoring goals (41 goals in 46 games), and Neymar made a decent start (15 goals in 41 games), but people were still waiting for the team to spark into life. And that would happen when Luis Suárez joined up in 2014.

At the 2014 World Cup in Brazil, the MSN trio, each playing for their home country, endured different fortunes. Suárez was off to a great start when he scored both goals for Uruguay against England in his team's second game. But then he lost control and bit an Italian defender. He was out of the tournament, and Uruguay soon followed.

Brazil's hopes were pinned on Neymar, who had led the national team to victory in the FIFA Confederations Cup in 2013 and seemed ready to guide his country to the biggest prize. Neymar scored four goals in three games in the group stage, and then the deciding goal in a penalty shootout against Chile in the round of 16. In the quarterfinal his team had a 2–1 win against Colombia, but Neymar suffered a violent foul near the end of the game and was badly injured. Without him Brazil was easy prey for Germany—suffering a demoralizing 1–7 defeat!—followed by the Netherlands.

Messi was also off to a cracking start, dragging a lackluster Argentinean team all the way to the final against Germany. But on the grand stage he could not summon his magic, and although Argentina was the better team, Germany scored the only goal. Messi was voted the player of the tournament, which was little consolation.

But the MSN trio had to leave the disappointments of the World Cup behind them. The serious prospect of a season at the Camp Nou awaited them in the fall of 2014.

Even geniuses sometimes fail. Messi's biggest wish was to bring the World Cup home to Argentina in the summer of 2014, but he failed to do so. Here Messi watches his dream slip away in the last moments of the final against Germany, on July 13, which Argentina lost without scoring a goal.

CAMP NOU

The stadium where the MSN trio went to work in the final summer days of 2014 is one of the world's largest and best equipped. It is called the Camp Nou, which simply means "new stadium." As an indication of how popular soccer is in Barcelona, 60,000 spectators showed up for the new arena's groundbreaking in 1954! When the Camp Nou was finished and unveiled in 1957, it could hold 106,000 fans. The stadium has expanded its capacity at times, including for the World Cup hosted by Spain in 1982 and for the 1992 Summer Olympics. Currently it has space for about 100,000 fans and is usually at full capacity at Barca home games.

Wembley stadium

EUROPE'S LARGEST

The Camp Nou has the largest capacity of any soccer stadium in Europe. It is followed by England's national stadium, Wembley, at 90,000. Among UEFA-approved stadiums, Westfalenstadion, in Dortmund, Germany, is third, holding over 81,000.

Camp Nou stadium

THE COACH

In the summer of 2014, Barça coach Gerardo Martino departed and a new coach arrived. The new man was known at the Camp Nou, but only as a player. Luis Enrique is from the city of Gijón in Spain's Asturias region, and started his career with local team Sporting de Gijón. He attracted attention for his combative midfield displays, and left for Real Madrid in his early 20s, playing there for five seasons. He did so well he nailed down a place on the national team, joining Barcelona man Pep Guardiola among others.

After running out his contract with Real Madrid, Luis Enrique elected to join the club's archrival, Barcelona. Very few have played for both teams, and even fewer have made the direct transition between them, but Enrique thrived in the new setting. He played for Barça for eight years and was one of the team's great players during that time. He was extremely versatile and could play most positions, but was at heart an attacking player, with a skill for goal scoring augmenting his aggressive and technically proficient play.

Enrique took over coaching duties at Barcelona B—the reserve team for FC Barcelona—from his friend Guardiola in 2008, but in 2011 he left for other prospects. He was, however, always bound to return, and in the summer of 2014 he became head coach of Barcelona's primary team. Initially Enrique's decisions about the lineup created tension among players, and by the beginning of 2015 rumors were flying that he and Messi were on a collision course. But the changes Enrique implemented worked out. He racked up the most wins for any coach that season, and Messi had a great year, as did Neymar and Suárez. Many fans think the coach's greatest achievement was his ability to have three awe-inspiring players in the attacking line and give each of them an opportunity to shine!

LUIS ENRIQUE
B. 1970
Played with Sporting de Gijón,
Real Madrid, and Barcelona
Games: 558
Goals: 144 (109 for Barça)
Games for Spain's
national team: 62
Goals: 12

MAJOR HONORS AS A PLAYER:

With Real: La Liga winner 1994–95
                     Copa del Rey winner 1992–93
With Barça: La Liga winner 1997–98, 1998–99
                     Copa del Rey winner 1996–97, 1997–98

Suárez, accompanied by Neymar and Messi, celebrates scoring Barcelona's second goal against Granada on February 28, 2015. The three teammates had ample opportunities to celebrate during the season.

MSN
The three superstars became known as MSN—their first initials run together.

Barcelona had a rocky start in the 2014–2015 season, and uncertainty seemed to affect the team. Luis Enrique had not yet convinced everyone that he was the right man to get Barça back on the winning path. Would he resurrect the famed tiki-taka style, or would his team play in a more direct manner? Would Leo Messi hit the heights again? How would the aggressive Suárez adapt to an attacking unit that was not built around him, as it had been at Liverpool? When Suárez was finally free from his ban, at the end of

October, the doubters seemed to have a point. Barça lost the first game after he returned, against arch-nemesis Real Madrid. The next game was another loss. Barcelona dropped to fourth place in La Liga.

In these games, Suárez had taken the right side of the front line, and Messi played the middle, his usual spot in recent years. But Messi suddenly returned to the right wing, where he had started his career. Supposedly this was Messi's idea: from the right he could gauge how to dictate play and make runs.

THE MSN TRIO

KICK OFF

infield. Suárez took the middle, and Neymar remained on the left.

As the season progressed, Barcelona's record improved, and Messi's zest for the game was revived. The forward players evolved into a stronger unit as they adjusted to one another's style of play. By playing farther back than he had in recent years, Messi was better able to direct the offense and thwart opposing defenses. Neymar was always ready with pinpoint passes or lightning-quick shots. And Suárez was

like a new person. He seemed calmer a more mature. He enjoyed playing amor teammates of equal brilliance, to whom could pass the ball whenever they were goal-scoring positions, instead of having do everything himself.

On March 8, 2015, Barcelona overtook Real Madrid at the summit of La Liga by thumping Rayo Vallecano. And when Ba won El Clásico (as matchups against Rea are called) two rounds later, it was obvic that the team was firing on all cylinders

THE CHAMP

Just as in La Liga, Barcelona got a slow start in the 2014–2015 group stages of the European Champions League, losing to Paris Saint-Germain (PSG) in their second match. But on November 5 in Amsterdam, against Suárez's former club Ajax, things started to click. This was the game in which Messi withdrew to the right wing, instructing his new teammate to play through the middle. This worked like a charm, and in the next game Suárez scored his first Barça goal, in a 4–0 win against APOEL from Cyprus. Messi scored the other three goals—and became the highest-scoring player in Champions League history, with 74 goals. But he and his teammates were not done yet. On December 10, Barça avenged its earlier defeat, trouncing PSG 3–1. Messi, Neymar, and Suárez scored one goal apiece. This was the first game in which all three scored, but this feat was to become a repeat performance.

In the next stages, Barça beat Manchester City fairly convincingly. Suárez scored both goals in a 2–1 away win, and his Croatian teammate Ivan Rakitić scored the only goal at the Camp Nou match. In the first game of the quarterfinals, Suárez was at it again,

landing two goals in a 3–1 victory over PSG. Neymar scored the third in that game and came alive in the second matchup with Paris, scoring both points in a 2–0 win.

With the front line performing like a well-oiled machine, Barça was on a roll. The first game of the semifinals was an outrageously easy win against world-class Bayern Munich, coached by Pep Guardiola, who could only shake his head at Messi's dominance. The Argentinean scored two goals and Neymar added the third in the 3–0 rout. Barça lost the second game, though it was almost a formality for the Catalan team, which had its eyes on the Champions League final.

Suárez celebrates after Messi has scored the first goal in the first semifinal game of the Champions League, against Bayern Munich, on May 6, 2015.

LA LIGA VICTORY

Barcelona players celebrate the national championship after the final game of La Liga on May 23, 2015, against Deportivo La Coruña.

Messi, Neymar, and Suárez were not the only players performing well in 2014–2015. Pedro was still playing an important role as understudy for the MSN trio and bringing in goals. In midfield, the tiki-taka maestro Xavi was certainly slowing down a little, but his comrade Iniesta was still in his prime. Sergio Busquets carried on unselfish work in defensive midfield, and Rakitić was fitting well into the team and scoring from midfield. In defense, Gerard Piqué was exemplary, and Javier Mascherano was at his combative best. But the three frontline players—the MSN trio—hogged the headlines, and deservedly so. Although Real Madrid went on a blazing run after losing the season's second El Clásico on March 22, the free-scoring MSN trio and their team were not to be caught. On May 17, Barça took to the pitch at the Vicente Calderón, the home stadium of La Liga's defending champion, Atlético Madrid. The home side defended tenaciously, but Barça clinched victory with a goal in the second half—scored by Messi, of course. So with a round to spare, Barcelona had won its seventh La Liga title in 11 seasons and its 23rd overall.

On the day Barça defeated Atlético in Madrid, one year had passed since Atlético had clinched the league championship for the first time in 18 years at the Camp Nou.

COPA DEL REY WONDER GOAL!

In Spain's Copa del Rey, or King's Cup, the MSN trio dominated. Their comrade Pedro was also an important force, tying Messi in scoring five goals over the course of the competition. The king of the Copa del Rey, however, was Neymar, who put away seven goals. The young Brazilian was growing ever more comfortable with his role and scored freely. Barcelona had several easy victories in the cup's first rounds, and then won a double against the strong Atlético Madrid team in the quarterfinal. Villarreal did not present much of a problem in the semifinal, and in the final, against Athletic Bilbao on May 30, 2015, Messi ruled the pitch once again. In a mesmerizing play, he received the ball on the right, near the center line, and shook off three defenders while storming toward the Basque team's penalty area. There, the Argentinean phenomenon spun a fourth defender around, and with two more Bilbaoans charging him, unleashed a swift shot at the near post past Athletic's helpless goalkeeper. It was a fantastic goal, one of Messi's best ever. Shortly thereafter, Messi unlocked the Bilbao defense by delivering a pass to Suárez, who unselfishly passed to Neymar, who scored easily. In the second half Messi ensured victory, making a neat goal with an assist from Dani Alves, who had acted on Neymar's quick pass. Barça's had its second cup in this amazing season! And the fight for the third was only a week away.

Messi leaves Athletic Bilbao player Mikel Rico behind on his way to scoring the opening goal of the Copa del Rey final on May 30, 2015.

Italian giants Juventus had reached the Champions League final for the first time in more than 10 years. The team had many famous names within its ranks, from the veterans Gianluigi Buffon, Andrea Pirlo, and Carlos Tevez to young guns Paul Pogba and Álvaro Morata. But with the MSN trio leading the line, Barcelona had to be considered the favorites. Midfield dynamo Rakitić scored the first goal, with an assist from Iniesta. Juventus fought back to tie the score early in the second half, but then the MSN forward line began tormenting the Italians. Suárez reinstated Barcelona's lead after Buffon failed to hold onto Messi's shot, and from then on it was all one way. Iniesta left the field after a virtuoso performance, making way for Xavi in his final appearance for Barça—one tiki-taka maestro for another. In extra time Neymar added a goal from a fast break. A fabulous season for the MSN trio had been completed.

KINGS OF EUROPE

Suárez, Messi, and Neymar celebrate with the European Champions League trophy.

European Champions League final match

June 6, 2015
Olympiastadion, Berlin, Germany
70,442 spectators

BARCELONA – JUVENTUS

3–1

GOALS

Barcelona: Rakitić 4'   Juventus: Morata 55'
Suárez 68'
Neymar

Barcelona's Lineup
Goalie: Ter Stegen
Alves – Piqué – Mascherano – Alba
Rakitić (Mathieu 91') – Busquets – Iniesta (Xavi 78')
Messi – Suárez (Pedro 96') – Neymar

Coach: Luis Enrique

45

GOALS IN THE FIRST SEASON

THE MSN TRIO'S FIRST SEASON, 2014–2015

- ⚽ La Liga
- 🏆 European Champions League
- 🏆 Copa del Rey

- ✅ Win
- ❌ Loss
- ➖ Tie

League		Date	Opponents	Result	Goals
⚽	✅	August 24	Elche	3–0	Messi 2, Munir
⚽	✅	August 31	Villarreal	1–0	Sandro
⚽	✅	Sept. 13	Bilbao	2–0	Neymar 2
🏆	✅	Sept. 17	APOEL	1–0	Piqué
⚽	✅	Sept. 21	Levante	5–0	Neymar, Rakitić, Sandro, Pedro, Messi
⚽	➖	Sept. 24	Málaga	0–0	
⚽	✅	Sept. 27	Granada	6–0	Neymar 3, Rakitić, Messi 2
🏆	❌	Sept. 30	Paris SG	2–3	Messi, Neymar
⚽	✅	Oct. 4	Vallecano	2–0	Messi, Neymar
⚽	✅	Oct. 18	Eibar	3–0	Xavi, Neymar, Messi
🏆	✅	Oct. 21	Ajax	3–1	Neymar, Messi, Sandro
⚽	❌	Oct. 25	Real Madrid	1–3	Neymar
⚽	❌	Nov. 1	Celta Vigo	0–1	
🏆	✅	Nov. 5	Ajax	2–0	Messi 2
⚽	✅	Nov .8	Almeria	2–1	Neymar, Alba
⚽	✅	Nov. 22	Sevilla	5–1	Messi 3, Neymar, Rakitić
🏆	✅	Nov. 25	APOEL	4–0	Suárez, Messi 3
⚽	✅	Nov. 30	Valencia	1–0	Busquets
🏆	✅	Dec. 3	Huesca	4–0	Rakitić , Iniesta, Pedro, Rafinha
⚽	✅	Dec. 7	Espanyol	5–1	Messi 3, Piqué, Pedro
🏆	✅	Dec. 10	Paris SG	3–1	Messi, Neymar, Suárez
⚽	➖	Dec. 13	Getafe	0–0	
🏆	✅	Dec. 16	Huesca	8–1	Pedro 3, Roberto, Iniesta, Adriano, Adama, Sandro

League		Date	Opponents	Result	Goals
	✓	Dec. 20	Córdoba	5–0	Pedro, Suárez, Piqué, Messi 2
	✗	Jan. 4	Sociedad	0–1	
	✓	Jan. 8	Elche	5–0	Neymar 2, Suárez, Messi, Alba
	✓	Jan. 11	Atlético	3–1	Neymar, Suárez, Messi
	✓	Jan. 15	Elche	4–0	Maieu, Roberto, Pedro, Adriano
	✓	Jan. 18	De. Coruna	4–0	Messi 3, SM o.g.*
	✓	Jan. 21	Atlético	1–0	Messi
	✓	Jan. 24	Elche	6–0	Pieué, Messi 2, Neymar 2, Pedro
	✓	Jan. 28	Atlético	3–2	Neymar 2, SM o.g.*
	✓	Feb. 1	Villarreal	3–2	Neymar, Rafinha, Messi
	✓	Feb. 8	Bilbao	5–2	Messi, Suárez, SM, Neymar, Pedro o.g.*
	✓	Feb. 11	Villarreal	3–1	Messi, Iniesta, Piqué
	✓	Feb. 15	Levante	5–0	Neymar, Messi 3, Suárez
	✗	Feb. 21	Málaga	0–1	
	✓	Feb. 24	M. City	2–1	Suárez 2
	✓	Feb. 28	Granada	3–1	Suárez, Rakitić Messi
	✓	March 4	Villarreal	3–1	Neymar 2, Suárez
	✓	March 8	Vallecano	6–1	Suárez 2, Piqué, Messi 3
	✓	March 14	Eibar	2–0	Messi 2
	✓	March 18	M. City	1–0	Rakitić
	✓	March 22	Real Madrid	2–1	Maieu, Suárez
	✓	April 5	Celta Vigo	1–0	Maieu
	✓	April 8	Almeria	4–0	Messi, Suárez 2, Bartra
	⊜	April 11	Sevilla	2–2	Messi, Neymar
	✓	April 15	Paris SG	3–1	Neymar, Suárez 2
	✓	April 18	Valencia	2–0	Suárez, Messi
	✓	April 21	Paris SG	2–0	Neymar 2
	✓	April 25	Espanyol	2–0	Neymar, Messi
	✓	April 28	Getafe	6–0	Messi 2, Suárez 2, Neymar, Xavi
	✓	May 2	Córdoba	8–0	Rakitić, Suárez 3, Messi 2, Pique, Neymar
	✓	May 5	Bayern	3–0	Messi 2, Neymar
	✓	May 9	Sociedad	2–0	Neymar, Pedro
	✗	May 12	Bayern	2–3	Neymar 2
	✓	May 17	Atlético	1–0	Messi
	⊜	May 23	De. Coruna	2–2	Messi 2
	✓	May 30	Bilbao	3–1	Messi 2, Neymar
	✓	June 6	Juventus	3–1	Rakitić, Suárez, Neymar

* "o.g." = own goal: indicates opponents scored in their own goal.

PRIVATE LIVES

Messi

has a girlfriend named Antonella Roccuzzo. She is from Rosario, Argentina, just as he is. They started dating in 2009, and on November 2, 2012, the first of two sons was born. He was given the name Thiago, which is the Spanish equivalent of Jacob. On September 11, 2015, Leo and Antonella welcomed their second boy, Mateo.

Luis

met Sofia Balbi when he was 15 years old, and it was love at first sight for both. Her family welcomed the boy into their home, but when Sofia's father was offered a job in Barcelona, the Balbis took the opportunity, moving across the ocean in 2003. Luis was determined to find a way to be with Sofia again. He worked hard in soccer training, aiming to get to Europe so that he could be closer to her. Luis and Sofia were married in 2009, and Sofia has stayed by her husband's side through good times and bad. They have two children: daughter Delfina and son Benjamin.

Neymar

has not (at this time) settled down with a lifetime companion. However, he does have a son, David Lucca, from a former relationship with Carolina Dantas. Neymar, who was 19 when David was born, said: "I cried when I heard that I was to become a father. At first, I felt fear. Then joy." Neymar described his newborn son as "2.8 kilograms [about six pounds] of pure joy." Neymar and Carolina have split up, but they help each other to raise the boy, and the soccer star loves being a father.

TEAMMATES

Although the MSN trio are Barcelona's most dangerous weapon, they are of course not alone on the team. A strong and unified squad has always been typical of Barcelona and still is. Some great players from the Guardiola period have departed, such as goalkeeper Victor Valdés and midfield general Xavi, and finally front man Pedro, but others have replaced them.

IN MIDFIELD

ANDRÉS INIESTA
Spain, midfielder, born 1984

Along with Xavi, he is the personification of the famous tiki-taka style. He has superb control of the ball, an exquisite eye for a pass, and makes the team interplay work. This is how he describes the Barcelona philosophy of focusing on technique and interplay, which he has mastered so completely: "Receive, pass, offer, receive

IVAN RAKITIĆ
Croatia, midfielder, born 1988

He did well for Basel, Schalke, and Sevilla clubs, but many doubted that this strong midfielder was in the Barcelona class. He proved his doubters wrong in his first season, fitting in well, scoring important goals, and fighting for the cause—and also showing a keen talent for the Catalan team's

SERGIO BUSQUETS
Spain, midfielder, born 1988

He is tall and a bit ungainly when compared to the nimble magicians on the field around him. In reality, though, he is a peerless presence in defensive midfield and more agile on the ball than he may appear to be.

SERGI ROBERTO
Spain, midfielder, born 1992

He emerged from Barcelona's academy and knows his skills, but he has yet to secure a place in the roster, which is overflowing with top talents.

RAFINHA
Spain, midfielder, born 1993

He may be in a similar situation to Sergi Roberto, but his talent is not in doubt. Rafinha's brother Thiago has joined Guardiola at Bayern Munich.

ARDA TURAN
Turkey, midfielder, born 1987

He arrived from Atlético Madrid in the summer of 2015. He is known for his strength and creativity on the field.

THE DEFENSIVE STALWARTS

MARC-ANDRÉ TER STEGEN

Germany, goalkeeper, born 1992

He played for Borussia Mönchengladbach before signing for Barça in 2014. During his first season he played in the Copa del Rey and the Champions League, did very well, and is considered a future primary goalkeeper.

CLAUDIO BRAVO

Chile, goalkeeper, born 1983

For many years he played for Real Sociedad in Spain but arrived at Barça in 2014; he was an ever-present contributor in the team's very successful season.

GERARD PIQUÉ

Spain, center back, born 1987

A local player who shipped off to Manchester United at the age of 17, he returned home in 2008 and soon became one of the best defenders in the game. Some thought he was in decline, but coach Luis Enrique has revived his career.

JORDI ALBA

Spain, left back, born 1989

A product of the Barça youth academy, he started his professional career at Valencia. He returned to Barcelona in 2012 and is known as an adventurous fullback.

JAVIER MASCHERANO
Argentina, defender, born 1984

A defensive midfielder turned by Guardiola into a central defender, he is an absolutely indefatigable warrior—one of the greatest soccer players in the world, although his contribution is not always highlighted. He arrived at Barça in 2010 and has appeared in more than 250 games.

DANI ALVES
Brazil, defender, born 1983

One of the most bold and entertaining fullbacks in the game, he enjoys himself much more on the attacking side of things. He came to FC Barcelona in the summer of 2008.

MARC BARTRA
Spain, defender, born 1992

A formidable defender, he has had, however, a tough time nailing down a place in the starting eleven, where competition is tough.

THOMAS VERMAELEN
Belgium, defender, born 1985

He made his name at Arsenal and moved to Barça in 2014, although he spent his whole first season injured.

JÉRÉMY MATHIEU
France, defender, born 1983

He was at Valencia for many years, but joined Barça in 2014 and has proved reliable in defense, in addition to scoring some vital goals in his first season.

COPA AMÉRICA 2015

Two of the MSN trio played a major role in the Copa América, the continental championship of South American nations, held in Chile in the summer of 2015.

LUIS SUÁREZ was suspended from the tournament, due to his ban from the previous year's World Cup. His absence was a contributing factor to the Uruguay national team's lack of success in the competition.

Messi consoles his teammate Gonzalo Higuaín after the latter missed a penalty in the 2015 Copa América final. Messi converted his own penalty shot with ease, but it was not enough.

NEYMAR captained Brazil and was expected to engineer the national team's rise from the ashes of the disastrous home-turf defeat at the World Cup the year before. This, however, did not go as planned. Without Messi and Suárez by his side, Neymar seemed to lack the maturity to shoulder the burden of his compatriots' great expectations.

He did get off to a good start, ensuring that Brazil beat Peru in the first game of the group stages by contributing a goal and an assist. In the next game, however, everything turned sour. Neymar and his teammates could not penetrate the rugged Colombian defense, and after the game Neymar received a red card for kicking the ball at an opponent in frustration. He made the situation worse by addressing the referee with foul language, getting himself a four-game competitive ban. Neymar was out of the tournament, and a disconsolate Brazil lost to Paraguay in the quarterfinals.

A CONSOLATION

Although the 2014 World Cup and the 2015 Copa América brought little but disappointment for the MSN trio, this is not all bad news for soccer fans. All three will be itching for victory in the next major tournament, the 2018 World Cup in Russia. It should be a sight to behold.

LIONEL MESSI was determined to make up for Argentina's disappointment at the 2014 World Cup final in Brazil, and initially seemed on course to do so. He was at the heart of Argentina's offense, and although things seemed to be moving in a positive direction, the strikers did not rack up many goals. Messi scored once, and the Argentineans needed a penalty shootout to overtake Colombia in the quarterfinal. But in the semifinal, the team turned on the style. Messi seemed at the height of his powers, boosting his teammates with assists so that Argentina beat Paraguay 6–1.

Sadly, the story of the previous year's final game was to repeat itself. Facing Chile, the Argentineans kept possession well, but the strikers failed, and Messi was unable to conjure up enough tricks to save the game. In the end, Chile won in a penalty shootout.

THE FOURTH CUP OF THE YEAR

The 2015–2016 season got off to a good start for the MSN trio at Barcelona, though August was a mixed bag. They had to accept a heavy loss to Athletic Bilbao in the matchup for the Spanish Super Cup. But they also captured the European (UEFA) Super Cup on August 11, 2015, in Tbilisi, Georgia. Barça, the leaders of the Champions League, met Europa League victor Sevilla, another team from Spain.

The game was incredibly entertaining. Sevilla took the lead after only three minutes, but Messi responded almost instantly and then scored again, putting Barça in the lead. The Catalans played a blistering first half, and extended their lead to 4–1 at minute 52. But Sevilla managed to make up its losses, and the game was tied at the end of the second half. Pedro, coming in at extra time, wrapped up the game with a goal in injury time. This was the great goal scorer's last one for Barça, as he was soon to join Chelsea. Pedro was reluctant to depart, but his prospects of playing regularly seemed slim with the MSN trio always ahead of him in the pecking order.

Barcelona's 2015–2016 uniform features hooped (cross-banded) jerseys rather than the familiar vertical stripes.

Suárez celebrates another goal with his teammates Sergi Roberto and Lionel Messi.

HOW TALL ARE THEY?

LIONEL MESSI
5' 7"

CRISTIANO RONALDO
6' 1"

NEYMAR
5' 9"

LIONEL MESSI
B. 1987
Has played only for Barcelona
Games 514
Goals 441
Games for Argentina 105
Goals 49

NEYMAR
B. 1992
Has played for Santos and Barcelona
Games 350 (125 for Barcelona)
Goals 213 (77 for Barcelona)
Games for Brazil 69
Goals 46

Size does not matter when it comes to soccer as it is easy to see. Neymar is among the tallest in the Barcelona squad, since many of the other important players on the team are less than six feet tall. Luis Suárez is 5 feet 11 inches, Mascherano is 5 feet 7½ inches, and Dani Alves is 5 feet 9 inches—just like Neymar.

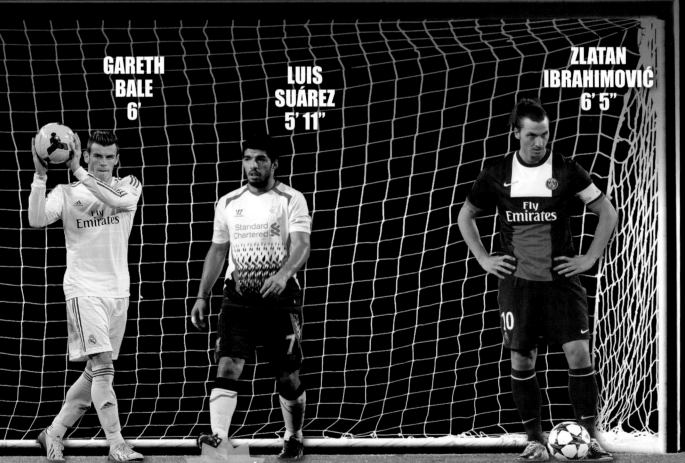

GARETH BALE
6'

LUIS SUÁREZ
5' 11"

ZLATAN IBRAHIMOVIĆ
6' 5"

LUIS SUÁREZ
F. 1987
Has played for Nacional, Groningen, Ajax, Liverpool, and Barcelona
Games 442 (81 for Barcelona)
Goals 285 (66 for Barcelona)
Games for Uruguay 82
Goals 43

AT THE TOP

On September 12, 2015, Barcelona met Atlético Madrid in La Liga. This was the first clash of the giants during the new season and was viewed as an indicator of the form of two of Spain's leading clubs. The stakes were high, as Real Madrid had clobbered Espanyol 6–0 earlier in the day, with Cristiano Ronaldo scoring five goals! Making it even more interesting, Messi was on the substitutes' bench. He had just arrived from playing for Argentina, and the day before Antonella Roccuzzo had given birth to their second son, Mateo. Messi had not slept much, and was therefore content to start this important game from the bench, although he usually insisted on playing each game. After a scoreless first half, Atlético exploited its home advantage with a goal at the beginning of the second. But the MSN trio stepped up the pace. Neymar scored with an exquisite free kick. Then Messi entered the match and scored the winning goal with a sneaky shot after an assist from Suárez. Barcelona was on top of the league!

A rare sight at the Vicente Calderón Stadium in Madrid: Lionel Messi on the substitutes' bench.

Pretending to suck his thumb, Messi dedicates a winning goal to his day-old son, Mateo.

OF COURSE, NO ONE KNOWS
WHETHER THE MSN TRIO WILL
STAY IN CATALONIA FOR THE REST
OF THEIR CAREERS. BUT THEY WILL
ALWAYS BE REMEMBERED AND
LOVED FOR THEIR EXTRAORDINARY
ACHIEVEMENTS—TOGETHER—
IN THEIR BARCELONA COLORS.